It's TRIATHLON Time

*Share the Journey together
as you find your finish line!*

BRIAN CLEVEN

FOREWORD BY MIKE REILLY
ILLUSTRATED BY BOBOOKS-EDD AND EREN

Brian Cleven

DEDICATION

To Amy, Natasha, and Kenzie,

The love and joy that you bring to my life drives me to make you proud in everything I do. You are truly my greatest blessings from God above!

Set Big Goals,
Work Hard,
And Get Them!

To my parents Russ and Kathy,
I could never Thank You enough for everything you have done for me. Your love and support have opened the entire world to me!

To friends and family,
Thank you for the joy you have brought to my life. You are loved and appreciated.
Never forget to enjoy the journey!

FOREWORD

"Embrace the Challenge: 'It's TRIATHLON Time'"

In a world where actions speak louder than words, "It's TRIATHLON Time" emerges as a powerful anthem for parents and children alike. In the heart of this book, Brian Cleven, an extraordinary father, embarks on a captivating journey, weaving the vital threads of participation, familial strength, and everlasting memories. With every stroke, every pedal, and every stride, he imparts an invaluable lesson – that the path to a powerful family bond is paved with shared experiences.

This book is more than a mere read; it's a transformational guide for all parents and their children. Its pages are a compass that will navigate you towards becoming an unbreakable family unit, bound by love, shared adventures, and the enduring legacy of togetherness. So, gear up and join the Cleven family on their inspiring journey. It's time for you to make a commitment to the most rewarding race of all – the race to become a stronger family, united by the unbreakable spirit of 'It's TRIATHLON Time.'

Mike Reilly, The Voice of IRONMAN

7

Today is your big day, Natasha. The two most important things to remember are to keep moving forward and to enjoy it! We did not tell you, but you get to run with Mommy today!
TEAM DADDY
777
TEAM DADDY

FINISH
Daddy, I did it! Just like you said I would. I got a little tired, but I made sure to pace myself. Check out my cool medal!
KIDS RUN
777
777

SWIM FINISH

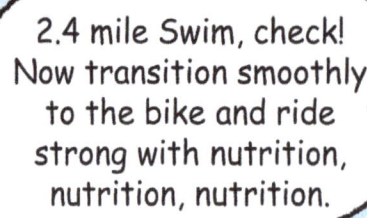

2.4 mile Swim, check! Now transition smoothly to the bike and ride strong with nutrition, nutrition, nutrition.

Oh wow! Mommy, Kenzie, Natasha!

We made it! And you are done with the part that worried you the most. You got this Daddy!

Go Daddy! Now just a long bike ride and a marathon with lots of friends!

23

ABOUT THE AUTHOR

Brian Cleven is a father, husband, 12-time full distance Triathlon Finisher and counting, and has run at least 1 continuous mile each day since July 2nd, 2010. From the small town of Peshtigo, Wisconsin he earned his bachelor's and master's degrees at the University of Wisconsin-La Crosse. As an ACSM Certified Clinical Exercise Physiologist and Licensed Athletic Trainer he leads a Cardiopulmonary Rehab program and performs Cardiac Stress Testing at the Bellin Health Marinette Clinic. In his free time, you will find him enjoying his family, traveling, training for his next race, or partnering with other community members to provide opportunities for people to become the healthiest versions of themselves!